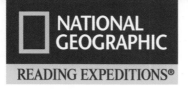

NATIONAL GEOGRAPHIC
READING EXPEDITIONS®

CHALLENGE AND CHANGE

The Big Catch

By Gare Thompson
Illustrated by Carlo Cosentino

Picture Credits
National Geographic Society; 7 (top to bottom) © Greg Smith/Corbis, © Jon Arnold Images/Alamy, © plainpicture/Alamy; 15, 25, 38, 46, 52 (diary art) David Cabot; 53 © Buddy Mays/Corbis; 54 © Jeff Greenberg/Photo Edit; 56 © Tim Bean/Corbis.

Produced through the worldwide resources of the National Geographic Society, John M. Fahey, Jr., President and Chief Executive Officer; Gilbert M. Grosvenor, Chairman of the Board; Nina D. Hoffman, Executive Vice President and President, Books and Education Publishing Group.

Prepared by National Geographic School Publishing
Ericka Markman, Senior Vice President and President, Children's Books and Education Publishing Group; Steve Mico, Senior Vice President, Publisher, Editorial Director; Francis Downey, Executive Editor; Richard Easby, Editorial Manager; Bea Jackson, Director of Design; Cindy Olson, Art Director; Margaret Sidlosky, Director of Illustrations; Matt Wascavage, Manager of Publishing Services; Lisa Pergolizzi, Sean Philpotts, Production Managers, Ted Tucker, Production Specialist.

Manufacturing and Quality Control
Christopher A. Liedel, Chief Financial Officer; Phillip L. Schlosser, Director; Clifton M. Brown, Manager.

Editors
Barbara Seeber, Mary Anne Wengel

Book Development
Morrison BookWorks LLC

Book Design
Steven Curtis Design

Art Direction
Dan Banks, Project Design Company

Published by the National Geographic Society
1145 17th Street, N.W.
Washington, D.C. 20036-4688

ISBN: 0-7922-5860-6

2010 2009 2008 2007 2006
1 2 3 4 5 6 7 8 9 10 11 12 13 14 15

Contents

The Dinh Family

The Dinh family lives in Galveston, Texas. The family runs a fish market, where they sell shrimp and fish caught by area fishermen. But with a new supermarket coming to town, their

Tina

Tina is 13 years old. Her full Vietnamese name is Van Tien Dinh, but she prefers to be called Tina. Tina's family is from Vietnam, but she thinks of herself as American. She loves to play basketball and write in her diary.

Tony

Tony is Tina's younger brother. His Vietnamese name is Tuyen Dinh. Tony is proud of his Vietnamese heritage. He likes to practice the cultural traditions of his family.

business may soon be in trouble. The Dinhs
face the challenge of new competition from
the supermarket and old prejudices from the
people around them.

Thanh and Hang Dinh

Thanh and Hang are Tina
and Tony's parents. They
run the family market and
work hard to support the
family.

An and Nguyen Dinh

An and Nguyen Dinh
are Tina and Tony's
grandparents. They
brought their family to
the United States from
Vietnam in the 1970s.
Nguyen once worked in
the shrimping industry.

The Southwest

This story takes place in the southwestern United States. The Southwest region includes four large states: Arizona, New Mexico, Texas, and Oklahoma. Fewer people live in the Southwest than in any other region in the United States.

SOUTHWESTERN STATES

- Arizona
- New Mexico
- Texas
- Oklahoma

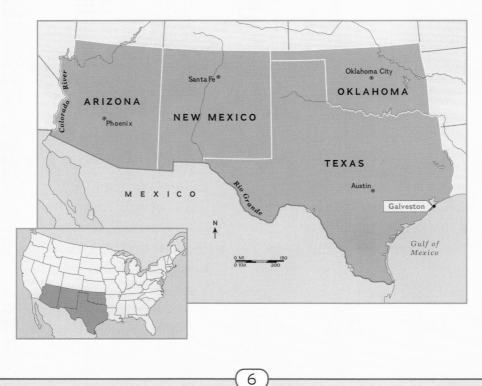

The Climate

The Southwest is known for hot and sunny weather most of the year. Storms in this region can be big. Hurricanes sometimes hit the area that is near the Gulf of Mexico. Tornadoes can threaten the flat land of Oklahoma and Texas.

The Location

Texas is the only state in the Southwest with a coast. It borders the Gulf of Mexico. The other southwestern states are all inland. Texas and Oklahoma have large areas of farmland and many ranches. New Mexico and Arizona have deserts and rocky canyons.

Industry

The Southwest is home to a variety of industries. These industries include oil production, tourism, ranching, and shrimping. It is common to see shrimping trawlers in the Gulf of Mexico, off the coast of Texas.

CHAPTER 1

November 2005

An American Girl

"Van Tien, it is time for breakfast. Come and eat before it gets cold," Tina's grandmother called. Tina sighed, she hated being called by her full name. Everyone else called her Tina.

Tina also hated eating a large breakfast. But she knew that her grandmother had prepared a breakfast of rice gruel, steamed fish, and vegetables. Her grandparents and parents ate it every morning, but Tina preferred cold cereal.

Her mother had explained several times that in Vietnam, breakfast was more like lunch here.

Tina wanted to scream, "Yes, I know, but we live in the city of Galveston, Texas, on the Gulf of Mexico, not in a small village on the Gulf of Tonkin in Vietnam!"

But she never did. Instead, she ate the rice dish every other day to avoid fighting with her grandmother. Tina wanted to show respect for all her family, but sometimes she wished her grandmother and grandfather lived in their own house and not with her family.

"I'm coming, Grandmother."

Tina raced down the stairs. Her younger brother, Tuyen, was almost finished with his breakfast. Naturally, he had eaten the **traditional** rice gruel and steamed fish. Tina shot him a dirty look. Why did he have to be so much like their grandparents? No wonder he had so few friends at school.

Tina, who was on the student council and played basketball, considered herself an American girl. Her brother was definitely more Asian. Sometimes she wondered if they were really brother and sister. But since they looked so much alike, she couldn't pretend she wasn't related to him.

---

traditional – an inherited or customary pattern of thoughts or actions

Tina bowed to her grandmother and sat at the kitchen table. Luckily, she had a granola bar in her backpack and could eat that on the bus. Tuyen laughed as Tina forced two bites of the gruel down her throat. She would get even with her brother later.

Her parents were at the fish store. They had left the house at the crack of dawn. "Where is Grandfather?" Tina asked.

"Oh, he is with your cousins, out shrimping. Your father needs more shrimp to sell in the store. Your grandfather is out trying to catch as much as he can."

Tina's grandmother smiled at the mention of her husband. It always amazed Tina that, even though her great-grandmother had arranged her grandparents' marriage, the two had fallen in love. Tina was happy that her family didn't follow the custom of arranging marriages anymore. She could not picture any of the local Vietnamese boys as someone she'd want to marry. Besides, she was too caught up in school and trying to win a scholarship for basketball camp. Marriage and boys were the last things on her mind.

Tina knew that some of her Vietnamese friends and cousins had marriages arranged at 16. Tina was glad that she was only 13. She also knew that her parents and her grandmother had dreams of her going to college and becoming a doctor. Tina sighed. It seemed almost all parents had dreams for their children that often had nothing to do with the kids.

Tina wanted to do something with sports, like maybe managing a team or becoming a sports agent. For now, to please her parents, she studied hard and got excellent grades in math and science, just in case she did have to follow their dream.

Tina ate one more bite of the rice gruel and then glanced at the clock. She realized that they would be late if they didn't move fast.

"Come on, little brother, let's go. The bus won't wait for us."

Before they had even gotten out the door, Grandmother began to clean the kitchen. Tina knew that she would clean the kitchen until it sparkled. Then she would pray at the shrine of the **ancestors** that the family had built and make

---

ancestor – a family member who came before

an offering. Tina wondered if she was as much a creature of habit as her grandmother. Tina hoped that she was not that predictable.

Tuyen, or Tony as his sister called him, bowed to his grandmother and told her to have a good day in Vietnamese. Tina smiled at her and kissed her goodbye. Her grandmother patted Tony on the head and kissed her granddaughter goodbye. Tina told her brother to hurry. Sometimes she wanted to leave her brother in the dust, but she knew that would be mean. Besides, Tony wasn't that bad. They reached the bus stop before the bus got there. Then Tony calmly sat down and crossed his legs in the lotus position. The other kids stared at him. Tina rolled her eyes and hissed, "Do you have to be so Asian? Everyone is staring at us. Well, at you." She moved away from her brother.

"I like being Vietnamese," he said, looking straight ahead. "It makes me different from the other kids." Tina knew he liked to clear his head before getting on the bus.

"It makes you different all right. I don't want to be different. I want to fit in." Tina frowned.

Tony looked at his sister, who was dressed from head to toe in American clothes. Except for her features, she looked like every other girl in school.

"Come on, here's the bus," Tina said. She jumped on the bus and quickly sat with her friends. Tony walked past her to the back, where he sat alone. None of his friends took the bus.

Tony watched his sister. They were so different. But Tony admired her. She was smart, a good athlete, and popular. So what if she resented being Asian in a white community?

Tony smiled as he remembered how Tina had stood up for him the first day of school. Some big kid had taken his new pencil case. Tony was proud of the case that his grandmother had made for him. Tina had walked up to the kid, who was twice her size, and demanded that he give it back. He refused at first, but when Tina didn't back down he handed it over. After that, the local kids left them alone. But by the time they reached middle school, Tina was more like them than she was like Tony. *Oh well, such is life*, thought Tony.

The bus passed their family fish store. Tony noticed that Tina stopped her conversation to see if she could spot their parents. Sure enough, both their mother and their father were standing in front of the store and waving at the bus. Tony smiled as Tina waved to her parents. *Family is family*, thought Tony.

Tina's Diary

November 18, 2005

All the kids at school were talking about Thanksgiving. Heather and Sandy are going to visit their grandparents. Heather is going to California. Sandy is going to Austin, the state capital. We don't celebrate Thanksgiving. My family has lived in America since the late 1970s, but we still don't celebrate all the holidays. Luckily, Maria Gonzales asked me to her house, and Mother said I could go.

Mother surprises me sometimes. She's more understanding than Father. Father seems worried these days. He has been saying that he has to get in more shrimp and lobsters for the holiday. He and mother had a quiet conversation about the fact that some of the fishermen will not sell their shrimp to us. It's because some laws were passed limiting the amount of shrimp that can be caught. Since then, some of the fishermen have been refusing to have anything to do with the Asian shrimp fishermen. I just wish we could all get along.

CHAPTER 2

Celebrating Tet Nguyen Dan

Tina wiped her brow. To her the house was clean, but obviously it was not clean enough for her grandmother or her mother. The three had been cleaning for what seemed like weeks. Well, it had only been one week. Tina grumbled under her breath as she washed the kitchen floor one more time. But she was really looking forward to celebrating the New Year, or Tet Nguyen Dan.

Tet was the most important holiday for the Vietnamese. All through January, Tina had watched the sky with her grandparents as they tracked the moon. Grandfather reminded the family that, if they were in Vietnam, they would be harvesting one crop of rice and then planting a new one. Of course, Tina did not bring up the fact that in Vietnam their family had not grown rice. They had been in the fishing industry.

At last the floor seemed to sparkle enough for both her mother and her grandmother. Tina looked out the window. Tony was climbing up and down the ladder, cleaning the windows.

Tina's grandfather was at the airport picking up relatives that had flown in for the Tet holiday. They had booked their flights into Galveston a year ago. Tina would be sharing her room with four cousins, while Tony would have five cousins sleeping in his room. Every room in the house would have relatives sleeping in it, either on couches or on the floor in sleeping bags.

Tina had to admit that she loved seeing her cousins from Massachusetts and California. They all talked about sports and boys. And Tony came alive during the holiday. Celebrating the holiday, Tony seemed to lose his quiet side. Among his cousins, he was often the loudest. Tina loved to see her brother laughing and joking, even if half of the time she did not understand the jokes he told in Vietnamese.

"Tina, help me distribute these flowers," Her mother said. "We want some in each room. You take the peach blossoms and the apricot flowers. I'll put the chrysanthemums in vases. Thank goodness, your cousin Lan sent these from California. Look, it is like we have spring in the house!" Hang Dinh loved the preparations for Tet, and Tina loved watching her mother get the house ready for the celebration.

"Tina, come help me string the lights," yelled Tony from outside.

"Sure, be right there," Tina answered. *For once, we're not fighting,* she thought.

Working as a team, they strung the colored lights all around the house. Tina's friends had asked why her family was putting up Christmas lights at the end of January. Tina had laughed and explained that the colored lights and red and pink banners were to celebrate the Vietnamese New Year.

Tina thought about Maria as they strung the colorful lights. Last year, Maria had asked if the

Vietnamese New Year was the same as the Chinese New Year. Tina had explained that the Vietnamese holiday was similar. Vietnam and China used the same lunar calendar, but the Chinese used the dragon in many of their parades. The Vietnamese celebration was quieter, with fewer fireworks and different foods. But many of the customs were the same. Both the Chinese and the Vietnamese gave children red envelopes filled with money on Tet.

Tina was happy that Maria was going to join them again this year. During the Tet celebration, Tina and her family ate sweet lotus seeds, winter melon strips, coconut, and kumquats. Her mother and grandmother had been shopping for the last month to find all the fruit that they needed. Tina wanted Maria to enjoy the Bahn Chung as she had last year. Maria had loved the sticky rice dumplings filled with beans and pork. She said they reminded her of the tamales that her grandmother made. Tina just hoped Maria would not feel odd with all her cousins chattering in Vietnamese.

"So, Tina, are you going to give up your basketball practice to stay home with the cousins?" asked Tony as he finished hanging the last strand of lights above the porch.

"No. I asked Dad, and he said I could still go. But he didn't really seem to be paying attention. I noticed that he, grandfather, and Uncle William have been talking a lot lately. What's going on?"

"Well, if you'd take your head out of your basketball hoop, you might realize that many of the local fishermen have not been selling Father as much shrimp and fish. They think that, since the law was passed that limited their catch, some of the Vietnamese fishermen should be restricted or even made to leave." Tony shook his head in disgust.

"Why do they think we should leave? We're Americans, too." Tina couldn't believe that people in the town would want her relatives to leave just because they were Vietnamese.

"In case you haven't noticed, we don't look like some of the Texan fishermen. And your good friend Heather's dad is the leader of the group that wants us out," Tony said.

"Heather's dad? But he's always been so nice to me at the basketball games."

"Think about it, Tina. Have you ever been to Heather's house? Has she ever been here? You only meet at school or at someone else's house."

Tina looked at her brother with new eyes. He was much more observant than she had thought. It had always bothered Tina that, whenever she asked Heather over, her friend always had an excuse why she couldn't come. Tina thought of Heather as a friend, but maybe what Tony said was true.

"Are we going to lose the store?" asked Tina. "Dad had been talking about expanding." How had she missed all this? She had to pay more attention to the conversations at dinner.

"No, the other Vietnamese fishermen still fish and sell to us, but there's a rumor that a new supermarket is going to open in town. If it does, Father is worried that we will have trouble competing if the locals won't sell their catch to him."

"I'm going inside to see if Mom needs help." Tina walked into the house. Suddenly, she realized how much she took for granted. They had a nice brick house in a good neighborhood. Their neighbors were white, Hispanic, and Asian. She thought that they were all friends. But maybe they weren't.

Tina went up to her mom and gave her a big hug. "What's that for? Mind you, I'm not complaining," Hang said, tucking Tina's long hair behind her ear.

"Is everything okay at the store?" Tina asked quietly. She didn't want her grandmother to hear her.

"It's fine. Why?"

"I was just wondering. I mean, Dad seems kind of worried."

"Oh, he wants to expand, but he's not sure the fishermen will sell him enough fish so that he can make a profit. And there are rumors that a big grocery store chain is going to open a store downtown."

"Will that hurt the store?" Tina didn't know what her parents would do if they lost the store.

"I doubt it. Our store has a fine **reputation,** and we have loyal customers. Plus, we give the fairest prices, both to buy and to sell."

"Does Heather's dad sell fish to our store?"

"No, he doesn't. But his sons want him to sell their fish to us. Your grandfather and father are going to a meeting of the shrimp fishermen. We'll see what happens." Hang looked at her daughter, wondering why Tina was suddenly so interested in the fish store. "Does that help?"

"Yeah." Tina decided to change the subject. "I can't wait for the holiday."

Tina thought that this New Year might even be more special than last year. She hadn't told anyone, but the coach said that there would be two spots open this year at the basketball camp in Houston. Tina would love to win one of the spots. But if there were problems at the store, there might not be enough money for her to go. Plus, one of her competitors for a spot was Heather.

-----

reputation – the quality or character of a person or business as judged by others

Before Tina could daydream about the future any longer, the doorbell rang. Then the loud voices of her cousins from California filled the house. Soon greetings enveloped Tina as she hugged her cousins and took their bags to her room. Everyone talked about the ceremony that would take place that night. The family would honor their ancestors. Her grandparents would pray at the altar and leave offerings of fruit and flowers. The smell of incense would fill the house. Tina liked the fact that her ancestors would "join" them for dinner that night. It made her family seem like a line of people extending back through time. *Maybe I'm not only American after all*, Tina thought.

Tina's Diary

January 31, 2006

I got $200 for New Year's. Not bad. Tony got the same. I think he thought he might get more because he participated in all the ceremonies while I went to basketball practice. But he didn't. At night when we lit a string of firecrackers, the police came to our street. Some of the people in town had complained. That has never happened before. We put out the firecrackers, but it put a damper on the festival. Maria came and had a good time.

I asked Heather if she wanted to stop by and she said no, she was busy. But later that day, I saw her out with her friend Patty. They were just hanging around. I think that Tony is right. Heather can't come over because of her father. I saw in the newspaper that he wrote a nasty letter about the Vietnamese in Galveston and how they were stealing all the good fishing spots from the locals. He said he wouldn't sell to a foreign store. Things are getting tense here. If that new supermarket opens, we could all be in trouble. Meanwhile, I'm practicing my jump shot and hoping that I'm better than Heather is.

The Deal

"Tina, could you please wait on Mrs. Phan?" Hang Dinh asked as she weighed some shrimp for another customer.

"Yes, Mother." Tina tried to put a smile on her face as she asked Mrs. Phan what she wanted.

Tina weighed and priced the sea bass as Mrs. Phan told her how she planned on cooking it. Tina was not interested in hearing how to deep fry sea bass and make an orange sauce to go with it. Tina wished that she were at school playing in the pickup game that had been her idea. But her parents had needed help at the store, and for once Tony was not able to help.

Tina knew Tony must have had something important to do, because he liked working at the store. He loved talking with the customers. In fact, Tony probably would have asked Mrs. Phan to write down her recipe for him so that Grandmother could try it. Tina wrapped Mrs. Phan's fish tightly in brown paper and then placed it in a plastic bag. Mrs. Phan thanked her and left the store.

Another customer asked for three pounds of the giant shrimp. As Tina waited on him, she noticed that the shrimp supply seemed awfully low. In fact, there was not quite enough to fill the customer's order. "Mom, do we have more shrimp out back?"

"No, that's it for today. We'll have more on Monday," Hang replied.

The customer looked annoyed. "Maybe I'll shop at the new supermarket when it opens. I'm sure they'll have plenty of shrimp," the man said.

"Oh, we will have plenty of shrimp. Don't you worry," Hang responded to the customer. "Please come back on Monday and you'll see."

Tina thought her mother sounded like she was almost pleading with the man. He took his shrimp and said he'd be back. Tina saw her mother's face relax with relief when the man said he'd return. *What is going on?* she wondered.

"So where are Dad and Grandfather today?" asked Tina.

"They are talking to the fishermen," Hang replied. "The big meeting was scheduled for this afternoon. They should be back soon. With the threat of the new supermarket and the falling price of shrimp, your father is hoping that many of the fishermen who would not sell to us before will do so now."

"Mom, are you sure our store is not in trouble?"

"Yes, Tina," Hang answered in her steady voice, "but you know that we want to expand. And we should do that before the new super-market opens. You know that things have been tense since the fishermen have been restricted in where they can fish and in the size of their catch. And, of course, relations have never been too easy between us and some of the local Texans."

"Why is that? I mean we're Americans, too. What is their problem?" Tina demanded. She did not understand it. She considered herself as American as her friends. In fact, some of her friends, such as Maria, weren't even citizens yet. "Why do the local Texan fishermen dislike the Vietnamese so much?"

Hang took a deep breath. "Well, in the early 1970s when immigrants like your grandparents came here, there were no laws restricting fishing. Many of the Vietnamese immigrants had been fishermen back home. So they worked and bought boats and started fishing for shrimp. Whole families worked on the boats."

"And you were just about my age then, right?" Tina asked.

"Yes," Hang said with a smile. "It wasn't so very long ago, though it seems like that to you. Anyway, we caught as much shrimp as the locals, if not more. We also took home more profits, because we weren't paying wages to family members to work the boats. And some of the Vietnamese fishermen fished in areas that the locals considered their territory. In some ways, they felt we were invading and taking their catch away from them."

"But, Mom, that was more than 30 years ago. Why do they still have hard feelings?" asked Tina, wondering how people could hold a grudge for that long.

"Some people just don't forget. Some locals went out of business and they blamed us." Then her mother laughed. "Let me give you an example. You know how Grandmother will not talk to Mrs. Phan?"

"Yes, I don't get that. I mean, Mrs. Phan shops here, and she's so nice."

"Well, years ago, in Vietnam, Mrs. Phan and your grandmother lived in the same village. To this day, Grandmother insists that Mrs. Phan stole a recipe from her and then used the recipe to try to win Grandfather."

"You have to be kidding me!" Tina burst out laughing. Somehow she couldn't picture women fighting over Grandfather. Granted, he was charming, but come on, he was no movie star.

"Yes, well, now you see how some people have long memories. Rather than letting the past go, they just relive it. So every time something bad happens, we often get blamed by the other fishermen. Just like your Grandmother has never forgiven Mrs. Phan."

At that moment, Tony ran into the store. For once, he was not quiet. In fact, he couldn't stop talking.

"Oh, man, you are not going to believe what happened at the meeting," he said, catching his breath. Luckily, there were no customers in the store, because it would have been hard to stop him.

"Tell us, tell us," Tina and Hang said at once.

"Well, we were all nervous because we knew that some of the fishermen resent us and always blame us when times are hard. But it was worse than we feared. When we walked into the meeting, the fishermen all gave us the silent treatment. Then they nudged each other and pointed at Father and Grandfather."

"Oh, that was mean," Tina said.

"Yeah, real mean," Tony said. "Sam Johnson, Heather's father, turned to his sons and said, 'Well, look what the cats dragged in. Don't you people know when you're not wanted?'"

"Heather's father said that?" Tina asked in disbelief.

"Yeah. One of her brothers tried to stop him, but he went right on. He said in a loud voice, 'These people are stealing our jobs.'"

"Oh, my," Hang said. "It got nasty."

"That's when Grandfather stepped in," Tony said. "First he placed his hand on Father's arms and they both bowed their heads quietly. Then he went to the front of the meeting hall and asked if he could speak."

"What did he say?" Tina demanded as their mother listened with wide eyes.

"He was great. He said, 'I am Nguyen Dinh and this is my son, Thanh Dinh.' He told them that Texas is our home, too, that we have been here a long time. He said that we are affected by the same rules and restrictions as they are."

"Good for Grandfather," Tina shouted.

"And then he proposed a plan," Tony said. "Listen to this: He said it would be better if we all worked together. He reminded them that the new supermarket will bring competition to all of us and that the supermarket buyers will probably get their fish and shrimp from Mexico, at cheaper prices."

"What was the plan he offered?" Hang asked breathlessly.

"That's what I'm getting to," Tony said. "The plan is this: Our store will pay the current price for their seafood and guarantee that price for a full year. Grandfather pledged to buy seafood from both white and Vietnamese fishermen. Everyone would have the same price."

"Wow!" Tina said. "That's pretty brave . . . and sort of risky."

"Grandfather said, 'We have a good business and many loyal customers. By working together, we can all make a good living.'"

"So what did the other fishermen do then?" Tina asked.

"They stopped glaring and started asking questions," Tony said. "Like, 'You'll pay the price we set?' That's when Father stepped in and said, 'As long as it is a fair price.'"

"Did they all agree to that?" Hang asked.

"Well, Mr. Johnson said a few more mean things, like 'How can we trust you people?'"

"I can't believe Heather's father is so awful," Tina stormed.

"Well, it didn't really matter by then," Tony said. "Everybody was nodding and saying that it sounded like a good deal. Then Father said, 'I ask you all to think about it.'"

"And then they just left?" Tina demanded.

"Yes," said Tony. "Then we all left the meeting. Father and Grandfather should be back here soon. They stopped to talk to Mr. Johnson's sons, who followed us out of the meeting. I don't know what happened."

"It's just about closing time," said Hang. "I think I'm going to close a little early. This is a lot to think about."

"Well, Mom, you better think fast. Here they all come now!"

Tina's father and grandfather walked into the

store, followed by Heather's two older brothers. Hang stopped wiping down the counters. She looked pale. Tina and Tony looked at each other and wondered what would happen.

"So, Mr. Dinh, you agree to pay us the current price?" one of the brothers asked. "Even if the new supermarket lowers their price?"

"Yes, you have my word," Thanh replied. "We will pay you the current price and continue paying that same price no matter what price the supermarket pays for their shrimp. Would you like me to put it in writing?"

The two Johnson brothers smiled. Then the taller one said, "No, it is about time we all started trusting each other."

"Yes, but what about your father? Will he agree to sell us your catch?" Thanh asked. Tina thought her father looked nervous but determined. Her grandfather was shaking his head as if he thought it would never happen.

"We will convince him. We have to work together on this, as you said, or we'll all be out of work."

"Fine, then start bringing me your catch next week," Thanh said.

Suddenly one of the brothers looked over at Tina. "Hey, aren't you on Heather's basketball team?" Tina nodded silently. "Heather says you're good."

"Van Tien is a fabulous player. She plays like Michael Jordan, except more gracefully," replied her proud grandfather.

"Well, I know Heather says that you are her main competition for one of the spots in the summer basketball camp."

"I think that Heather will get it. She's out there practicing now," Tina shrugged. She honestly thought that she had an equal chance at the spot but wasn't going to admit that to Heather's brothers. Tina knew that her father had worked hard to work out the deal with Heather's brothers and didn't want to blow it.

"Hey, she's good, but don't give up. A little friendly competition is a good thing." The boys shook hands with her father and grandfather and left.

Hang went over and hugged her husband. That surprised Tina. Her parents never showed affection in public. Then, to her total amazement, her grandfather gave her a high five. Tina laughed. Her parents told her she could go practice basketball. Tina thanked them. If she raced home and changed, she would be able to make it in time to play in the pickup game at the school. She'd show Heather who had the moves.

Tina's Diary

April 1, 2006

Well, it's no April Fool's joke; things seem to have settled down here in Galveston. I don't think that my dad and Heather's dad will ever be friends, but maybe Heather's brothers can convince their dad to sell us shrimp.

Boy, Heather is one great player. She has a terrific jump shot. I'm a better defensive player, but I think she will beat me at tryouts.

My dad told me a story about Heather's family. In the 1970s her father was a wild teen, and he and some of his friends plotted to burn some immigrants' boats. He never did, but his pals did. One Vietnamese man almost died. His friends got caught. Ever since then, Heather's dad has resented all the immigrants because he believes that they ruined his friends' lives. I guess Heather's dad never read any Confucius. If he had, he would know that each man is responsible for his own actions. Well, at least we've made a little progress. We don't have to worry about the locals burning down our store. At least, I hope not.

The Illness

Tina sat in the waiting room of the doctor's office with her mother and grandmother. They had taken her grandfather to the hospital a few weeks ago because he had a cough that he could not seem to shake. He had tried different herbs and had seen an **acupuncturist**, but none of the normal remedies seemed to work. Over-the-counter medicines had failed, too.

---

acupuncturist – a person who uses needles to puncture the body at specific points to cure disease or relieve pain

Now they were in a doctor's office. The doctor specialized in cancer. Tina's whole family had been trying to avoid the word *cancer,* but there it was. Grandfather had lung cancer. Tina's grandmother shook her head and said that he had never smoked but all his friends smoked heavily. On the boat he had breathed in all that smoke all those years.

Tina thought back over the last few months. The family had made several offerings to the ancestors to look after Grandfather. But still he had not gotten better. Then the x-rays showed a small spot on his left lung.

Tony had researched lung cancer on the Web. He found information about the disease. He also found remedies that Eastern doctors use to help Grandfather feel more comfortable with the treatment. Everyone knew that Grandfather did not really believe that Western medicine was any good. But Dr. Steinberg seemed to believe in using both Eastern and Western methods to cure cancer. Somehow the doctor had made Grandfather feel safe. So now the family was awaiting the verdict.

Suddenly Tina's thoughts switched to the present. Tina knew that, right now, Heather was trying out for the summer camp spot. Tina's parents had said she should go to tryouts, but she knew that she had to be with her grandfather. Tony had to work at the store, so she had to be here. Tina leafed through a magazine, not really focusing on any of the stories. Her mother took the magazine out of Tina's hands. "Why don't you take a walk?" Tina smiled at her mother and got up.

Outside, the fresh air felt good. Tina sat down under a tree and was glad to be out of the hot Texas sun. As she leaned back against the tree, a cool breeze brushed her face and seemed to take away her worries. Tina drifted off to sleep. Then she heard her name being called.

Tina ran to her mother. "Well?"

Hang hugged her tightly. "It looks good. Grandfather will have to have radiation, but not chemotherapy. The doctor thinks that they got it all. We are lucky. We have to bring Grandfather and Grandmother to the temple. They want to say a prayer and make an offering and give thanks for our good fortune."

"Of course, let's go." For once, Tina wanted to join in her family's rituals.

After her grandparents had made their offering, the family went to the store. Tina rushed in to tell her father and brother the good news. "He's going to be fine. Grandfather is going to be fine."

"Ah, it was my green tea and other herbal remedies. I knew that they would work," Tony proclaimed. Tina playfully punched her brother. "Maybe it was. But who cares what worked, as long as it did."

Once everyone had stopped talking and calmed down, Tina noticed that her grandfather looked gray and tired. "Grandfather, you should

go home and rest." Normally, Grandfather would tell Tina not to worry or to mind her own business, but he just smiled and nodded. Her grandmother said he needed to sip some rice gruel and go to bed. Hang took them home. Tina stayed at the store.

"So, you missed the big tryouts, huh?" asked Tony. He tried to keep his voice low, but Tina's father heard him.

"The tryouts were today? Why didn't you go, Van Tien?" Her father looked concerned.

"I couldn't leave Grandfather. I wanted to be there. Besides, hearing the news about Grandfather was better than winning a scholarship."

"Perhaps you can go to camp anyhow?"

"Oh, Dad, it's really expensive, and expanding the store is costing a lot. We don't have the money."

Tina had heard her parents talking about how they were short with money. But they had finished the expansion before the new supermarket opened. So far things seemed to be working out. Heather's brothers had convinced their father to sell shrimp to Tina's dad, and now Mr. Johnson even said hello to her family when he saw them in town. He'd come a long way. Tina remembered that he used to cross the street when he saw an Asian person walking toward him.

"I think that we should have a family conference and talk about it," Thanh said in a very serious voice. Tina looked at her brother, but Tony just shrugged and mouthed that he had no idea what her father was talking about.

Tina stayed at the store until it closed, and then the three drove home in silence. For once, the silence did not bother Tina. She knew that her brother was off in his meditative world and her father was thinking. Tina did not need her usual music blaring out of the radio. She wondered if Heather had made the team. Tina bet herself that Heather had.

When they arrived home, Grandmother cooked a special meal. They had fried sea bass with orange sauce, crispy noodles, and steamed dumplings. They toasted Grandfather with green tea. Grandfather said he missed his plum wine. Grandmother just smiled and poured him another cup of tea. After the meal, Tina helped her brother do the dishes.

"I'm sorry that you didn't get to try out." Tony did look sad.

"Oh, it's fine. As long as Grandfather is going to get well, that's good enough. It would have been fun, but there's always next year. Think how good I'll be next summer."

Tina's Diary

June 6, 2006

I heard from Heather, and she got a scholarship. She said that I would have if I had tried out. She was glad to hear about my grandfather. She's coming over tomorrow. She said that her father has told her how honest and fair Dad is, and he is glad to sell us shrimp. Well, he should say that because it's true.

I looked up some old newspapers on the Web. Things here were bad when Grandfather and his family first arrived. It must have been rough for Dad. He came here on a boat and almost died getting here. Then the family didn't speak English. All they knew how to do was to fish for shrimp.

The locals resented the Vietnamese fishermen because they worked so hard and sold their shrimp for less. Dad says he owes it to the local men to buy their shrimp at a fair market price (whatever that means!). I'm just glad that it all worked out. The old newspaper accounts told about boats burning, people's homes being set on fire, and families losing everything. Thank goodness times have changed. Maybe good luck is here to stay.

The Good Luck Holds

Tina woke to a beautiful June day. School was almost out. She no longer felt bad about having missed the chance to try out for summer camp. There would be another session in July. Maybe she would try out then, though most of the scholarships were only for the first session.

At least things were going well at the store. Tina had to smile. Tony, of all people, had said that they needed to paint the store a bright color, such as lucky red, and decorate it with shrimp.

Tina thought he had lost his mind, but the new paint made the store look great. And you couldn't miss it from the road.

"Van Tien, it is time for your breakfast. Come down," her grandmother called.

Some things never change, thought Tina, as she threw on her clothes. Her grandmother would always be there to call her for breakfast. Tina smiled. And her grandfather would be there reading the paper and making silly jokes. His cancer was in remission. Tina shrugged. Maybe all those offerings to the ancestors and drinking the green tea had helped.

"Van Tien, come here now!"

Or maybe the powers that be just didn't want to deal with Grandmother's wrath.

"I'm coming, Grandmother." *It's a rice gruel day,* thought Tina.

Tina rushed downstairs. Nobody was in the kitchen. Everyone was standing in the dining room behind her place.

"Why aren't you at the store?" Tina asked her mother and father. "What's going on?"

"Just sit down," ordered her grandmother.

Tina sat. She knew better than to argue with her.

Then Tina looked down. At her place was a bright, cut-up orange, and under it was a large red envelope. Tina picked up the envelope. "What's this? It's not a holiday or my birthday. What's going on?" But no one spoke.

Finally, Tony broke the silence. "Oh, just open it. Stop playing Twenty Questions."

Tina opened the envelope. She pulled out a letter of admittance to the summer basketball camp. Tina started screaming with joy.

"Tina, not so loud," yelled Grandmother as she hugged her. Soon everyone was talking, so Grandfather held up his hand.

"You have a dream, so we decided you should achieve your dream. You always help your family at the store, and you are good friends with Heather, whose father finally decided to sell us shrimp. He tells us he thinks that you are a good player. Heather needs you on the team to keep up her game, so you are going."

Tina didn't know what to say. It was so amazing. Her mother and father kissed her on the head.

"It's time for us to get going," Tina's father said. "Come on, Tony, it's your turn at the store. You need to help us finish the Web site." Tony winked at Tina as the three of them left.

"I am going to the dock to talk to the fishermen. I think they need my advice," Grandfather said. And then he disappeared.

"This is so cool, Grandmother," said Tina. She could barely breathe. She was so excited.

"Here, you eat your breakfast." Her grandmother put down a dish of cold cereal.

"Where's the rice gruel?" asked Tina.

"What, you don't like cereal? It's good for you. Eat." Her grandmother sat down with her. Tina started eating and then she noticed something. Grandmother was not wearing her gold and jade bracelet.

"Where's your bracelet?"

"Oh, that old thing. I sold it."

Suddenly it dawned on Tina: Grandmother had sold her prized bracelet to help pay for basketball camp.

"We have to get it back. I won't go to camp," Tina said, starting to cry.

"No, Tina. You become a doctor and then you can buy me lots of bracelets." Her grandmother hugged her. "Now finish eating so that you can practice."

Drying her tears, Tina ate her cereal. Maybe she would become a doctor. She could major in sports medicine. She'd have to talk to Tony about it. And if she worked hard enough, maybe she could combine her wish to work in sports and her grandmother's wish for her to become a doctor. *Life is full of deals and compromises*, Tina thought as she beamed at her grandmother and finished her cereal.

Tina's Diary

June 9, 2006

Talk about good luck! I get to go to basketball camp after all! I was going to help Heather practice this weekend so she would be ready for camp. Now we can practice as teammates!

My family surprised me with a special breakfast and a letter from the basketball camp. Grandfather said I deserve to go because I help out at the store so much and because Heather's father said that I am a good player. But I help out at the store because I am a part of the family. I am good at basketball because I work hard at it. Working hard is something I learned from my family. I am proud of how hard they work.

My family made many sacrifices to come to the United States. Now my parents and grandparents make sacrifices for Tony and me. Grandmother even sold her beautiful bracelet so that I can go to basketball camp. I hope she knows how much I appreciate it.

One thing I've learned this year is that even though I think of myself as an American, I am very happy that I can also be Vietnamese.

Life on the Gulf Coast

Galveston, Texas, is located on the Gulf of Mexico. The city has a big port and is a center of the fishing and shrimping industries. Many people from Mexico, Europe, and Asia have settled in Texas. Many Vietnamese have moved to the Galveston area. They often work as fishermen and shrimpers.

Shrimp

Shrimp are small sea creatures with a thin shell, 10 legs, and a tail. Many people around the world enjoy eating shrimp, so fishing for shrimp is a big industry.

Catching shrimp

Shrimpers, or people who catch shrimp, work from a boat called a shrimping trawler. The boat drags long net bags along the bottom of the ocean to snare the shrimp. The shrimp are kept on ice until the boat returns to shore. A shrimping trawler may be out on the water for up to three weeks at a time.

The Vietnamese in Texas

Vietnamese immigrants came to Texas starting in the late 1970s. They faced many difficulties. Most did not speak English, so they had a hard time finding work. Some families opened restaurants or stores in their communities. Other people became fishermen or shrimpers. Today, many Vietnamese Americans still work as shrimpers in the Gulf of Mexico.

Celebrating Tet Nguyen Dan

Tet Nguyen Dan is the most important Vietnamese holiday. This celebration takes place in late January or early February. Also known as Tet, it marks the start of a new year. People work hard to get ready for Tet. They clean and paint their houses and decorate with flowers. They buy new clothing, and they prepare traditional foods to share with family and friends.

Write a Personal Letter

In the story, Tina is facing a time of challenge and change. Imagine that you are Tina's friend and you are going to write her a letter.

- Copy the chart below.

- In the first column, list some of the challenges Tina and her family are facing in the story.

- In the second column, list possible ways to face these challenges. Use information from the story as well as other sources.

- Use your completed chart to write a letter to Tina. Offer your advice and encouragement to help her deal with the challenges she faces.

Challenge	Ways to face the problem
1. The family store does not have enough shrimp to sell.	1. Make a deal with the fishermen to always offer a fair price.

Read More About the Southwest

Find and read more books about the Southwest. As you read, think about these questions. They will help you understand more about this topic.

• What are the southwestern states?

• What are some of the cultures and traditions that make up the Southwest?

• What are some of the important industries in the Southwest region?

• What are some natural resources found in the Southwest?

• What are some physical features of the land in the Southwest?

SUGGESTED READING
Reading Expeditions
Readings About America:
The Southwest Today

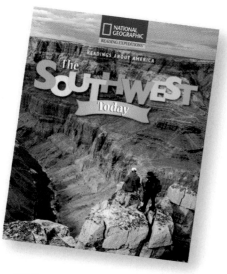